The Shadow of a Dog
I Can't Forget

Poems & Prose

MARY KENNEDY EASTHAM

To GOD- MICHAEL & JOE—
YOU ARE SWEET,
BEAUTIFUL & SO MUCH
FUN.
♡ YOU
MARY

E-MAIL: marylovesdogs @sbcglobal.net

Robertson Publishing
59 N. Santa Cruz Avenue, Suite B
Los Gatos, California 95030 USA
(888) 354-5957 • www.RobertsonPublishing.com

ACKNOWLEDGEMENTS

A special 'THANK-YOU' to the very generous ARTS COUNCIL OF SILICON VALLEY who gave me several writer's grants, to the DOROTHY SARGENT ROSENBURG FOUNDATION, a group of caring individuals who wholeheartedly believe that the world needs more great poets, to the NATIONAL LEAGUE OF AMERICAN PEN WOMEN, an invitation-only writer's organization who sponsor countless writing contests and especially EILEEN MALONE who nearly a decade ago asked me to be a judge in the SOUL-MAKING LITERARY COMPETITION, a contest that has taught me so much more about writing than I could ever have learned on my own, to JUNE COTNER for selecting my poetry for a number of her beautiful anthologies to include FAMILY CELEBRATIONS, WEDDING BLESSINGS and MOTHERS & DAUGHTERS, to RICK LUPERT of the POETRY SUPERHIGHWAY who was the kick-in-the-pants for me putting this collection together, to the MAP OF AUSTIN POETRY who published a number of my early poems and to the many other contests and venues that either published my work or gave me money (and in the best of circumstances did BOTH!) It is because of all of you that I now have a legitimate résumé and have been able to create for myself a writing life. Thank-you Pat Rotondo for making BY HAND the elegant, ONE-OF-A-KIND First Edition of 'Shadow of a Dog I Can't Forget', a copy of which went on to become a BEST BOOK winner in the 2005 USA BOOK NEWS contest. Thank-you Trish and Wendy for never saying 'No' when I asked you to look at my most recent work, sometimes for the seventeenth time! Thank-you to my family and friends all over the country who continue to nourish me and believe in me. Thank-you, Karen for having a playful life I can steal from. Thank-you Sandy and Ginny and Holly and Katie and Carol and Jan for always having a listening ear. Thank-you to my early teachers Thaisa Frank, Kate Braverman and Annie Lamott who said my work showed promise in the days when I was terrified to do even one rewrite. By sharing their magical gifts for storymaking with me, these talented women gave me the courage to write from a position of authority. Thank-you M.J. Rose, author and writing coach whose on-line 'BUZZ YOUR BOOK' course helped me fill in the missing pieces so that an even better Second Edition of 'Shadow of a Dog I Can't Forget' could be birthed. Thank-you to my beautiful dogs without whom I COULD NOT LIVE and thank-you Mark for continuing to walk the streets of love with me every day. 'I love you, baby.'

For Jack - my Best Boy
June 16, 1993 – November 3, 2003

We can never know what to want,
because, living only one life, we can neither
compare it with our previous lives
nor perfect it in our lives to come.

MILAN KUNDERA
The Unbearable Lightness of Being

The blood jet is poetry.
There is no stopping it.

SYLVIA PLATH

No matter what I say, I will never discover
why one writes and how one doesn't write.

MARGUERITE DURAS
Writing

TO THE READERS

My horoscope recently said stop hugging the shadows, step back into the limelight. I'm shocked by how accurate it is. I've struggled with this paradox all my life. I am the good girl, the popular loner. I am the quirky girl, the glamorous independent spirit. I want, I crave love but I also need my freedom. I want, I crave attention and yet at times I must retreat, stepping back into the shadows. The only way I've found to reconcile this is to become a word actress letting my characters perform different roles on paper which is of course weaving my own needs, my own fantasies, my love, my loss and my joy into the poems and stories I write.

What do I hope you will get from reading my work? Hafiz says a poet is someone who can pour light into a cup and then raise it to nourish your beautiful – perhaps parched – holy mouth. Take me into you…relax into my storied world…Enjoy…

CONTENTS

Is there ever such a thing
as a tiny betrayal?

'Do you close your eyes when you kiss?' he asks me.
He's left the hotel door half open. Someone looking in would see
bare legs dangling from a persimmon and gold chaise, my
platinum silk high heels ready to walk, or not.
'I'll ruin you if I stay," I say.
"Stay," he says this beautiful man with the easy smile.
'Kiss me badly,' I plead, my eyes closed to other nights I knew,
me being the girl men fall in love with and then try to change.
Off in the distance I imagine the beauty of words
as they fall from the mouths of my babies, just now being put down
to bed.

The Soul of a Red Rock

I first saw your rim shadows
backlit by lightning.
You bled beauty
against the cloak of the thunderstorm's rage.
I didn't question how you got there
what forces came together in your birth.
Instead I watched you change
with the wind's firesong
holding close
destiny's searchlight.

Breaking Them In

He's come back to these hills
to break in new boots
at least that's what he says.
Through prairie winds and days full of hot sun
he walks, wondering if the trodden weed
has held it in — all of it — the voices, the faces
the conversations of his past.
From the tip of a trembling hill
the deer appears
not the one his father made him kill
this deer has dark eyes that do not turn away.
He can see it now so clearly
his mother's hat on the garden swing
fallen apples on the steps
the deer unafraid, content to chomp.
The next day, apples mixed with blood
below the carcass.
It happened in the gloaming
not night, not day, somewhere in between
when the air feels draped in silk
tossed across a bead-edged sky.
Bad things shouldn't happen
in that time of perfect light.
He finds himself not going to pieces
as he thought he would
boots loosening on his feet.

The Making of Names

She uses cotton balls
to dry the wings of insects
after a rainfall.
An eggplant can lay cradled in her arms
like a friend's new baby
until that moment when WHACK
she cuts through it
with a long, sharp knife.
Who gets to decide, she often says
if this is less than love.

Friends for a time, two small-town girls
living in furnished studio apartments
you'd never let your grandmother see.

We wanted more.

On those stillborn L.A. afternoons
when we couldn't find work,
we'd make up stories about our neighbors,
tiny binoculars tied with cheap string
around our necks. We called our game
the making of names.

Lola Montana drops her dryer-hot thongs on dirty wooden stairs
waiting for 30-something Rick Spendlove,
a cute guy with braces and a broken foot
to return them.
Fiona Fatalle has NO EXPECTATION tee-shirts in every color.
Sara Easy prefers men wearing bands of gold
that scream like sirens through flushed beams of sun.

The day after we painted horses
on the pool's empty bottom,
my friend slipped a good-bye note under my door.
She signed it 'Amy", her real name,
a name she'd never used before.

Find the Men Who Killed the Horses

The day is warm for December
but the Reno sun has dead eyes.
Ten miles outside of town
two men, Marines, with high-powered rifles
go on a rampage
killing 34 wild Mustang horses
who can't imagine
a death more brutal.
I want to ask the men
what they did
as these horses ran out of breath and time.
I want to ask the men
to describe for me
the sound of a Mustang's final wail.

When they find the men who killed the horses
(and they will)
I will tell them this is war
they must strip naked
while I use a mop to cover their bodies in Mustang blood.
I will ask them to put their ears to the cold ground
and listen for what shall never again be.
And then I will set them free
in the fields
where the Mustangs knew nothing
but peace and freedom
and I will whisper to the bobcats
'Go on, find them, find the men who killed the horses'...

Terrorism
(As seen through the eyes of a little boy)

In the doorway a gun tip's shadow
points toward his face.
Yesterday he saw death
along a railroad track.
Two heads. Four bodies. One arm.
Expect a storm before nightfall
the soldier tells him,
I want a piece of bread with butter
I want to take a nap.
'Only fools hear the rhythm of war's rhapsody'
his uncle yells from upstairs.
'Run, run,' the boy tells a stray dog
perched in the alleyway
where his family once gossiped.
He doesn't flinch when a storefront window explodes
all too familiar with the geography
of fractured glass.

As the setting sun drapes a curtain
across a hundred little hatreds,
stunned pigeons scatter toward the heavens
like a handful of black umbrellas.
He draws a bunny in the dirt with his toe
circle ears, circle face, square belly, a long craggy tail.
The soldier starts to erase it, then doesn't
praising him for knowing
how to stay within the lines.

Malibu

Cover me in your wet wash
passionate waves
edge of the sky wild
tethered to nothing
in this sunset froth
but your love's thunder.

Clouds

It wasn't until today I wished him dead.
He can't swallow, can't remember who I am.
On our afternoons together I bring him lollipops
like the ones he carried in his bathrobe pocket
for the nights he found me sleepwalking
my fluffy bunny slippers covered in mud
and me dazed, not knowing where I was.

In sixth grade he told me clouds
were the dreams we hadn't yet thought of.
I kiss his rootbeer lollipop lips
take off his socks, his shoes
lay him down on the warm grass
my sweater as his pillow.
My father was always comfortable with himself.
I take his hand, tell him to grab hold
of an imaginary ladder made of twisted vines and love.
'Up we go, Daddy,' I say 'higher, higher'
as I give him back the clouds.

Points of Love

The storm was unexpected
New Yorkers swept inside by snow.
In 4B a woman bathes her lover
careful not to wet his broken hand.
The Egyptian newlyweds
living in the building's only studio
give their dreamchildren names
underneath a tent of bedsheets.
Twin sisters, designers, in Versace mules
play spin-the-bottle
on their penthouse terrace
with models from Milan.
Alone in her garden apartment
a Venezuelan widow
listens to vinyl records
she once danced to
with her husband.
And outside, on the street,
as the snow unfurls around them
like a ream of white velvet
let loose,
a girl in a scarf
the color of blood red calla lilies
says 'yes'
to a proposal of marriage
while riding on the turned up handlebars
of her lover's rusty Schwinn.

16 Parisville Place

She likes the number, same as her age
puts all her hope behind the bright red door.
Pretty things will hang in her walk-in closet here.
Guns won't fire. There will be no need to hide
foster brothers and sisters in another
cold white porcelain tub, her own feet
quivering on the toilet seat
as she searches for shadows in the thin line of light
beneath the locked bathroom door.
She knows there are other places, places that will take her in
but she is tired, tired of announcing to another blank face
Pearl Alice is my birth name but you can call me Fancy.
The realtor drives up, smacks a SOLD sign over PLEASE COME IN
she doesn't see Pearl Alice sitting on the curb across the street
doesn't leave a key for her
underneath the mat.
I wish none of this were true.

What Marilyn Says
About Her Things Being Auctioned

It wasn't enough to fill my lips with booze and pills
lay me down, enter me, then dress me back up.
You still want more,
I say it's time to let go of 'The Monroe'.
I'd blow the rhinestones off that Happy Birthday dress anyway.
Give it to Pamela Lee.
She seems to be making the same bad choices I did.

The PETA people will be all over
whoever buys the suit I wore to marry Joe.
I kept the white mink collar in cotton balls for years.
It's gotta smell.

I'm happier now.   11
No need for false eyelashes or dark scarves
on the days my hair needs coloring.
I walk around naked
but where I am, we all do.
Jackie and I formed a book club, like Oprah's.
This month's selection is 'The Madonna/Whore Complex.'
Check out our website for future listings
www.jackie&marilyn.stillholdingon.

Untitled

She was my one good thing that got taken away.
Her daddy was a traveling radio preacher who nailed me
in his chapel, a beat-up Land Cruiser
plastered with bumper stickers most truck stops
couldn't give away.
We were like Jewel in her early days
car-bound and poor.
On the road, late at night, he covered me
in plastic bags from Wal Mart, our love blanket
told me I was his inspiration
which is why I didn't see it coming
me, the axed tree falling to her death.
His sister was waiting for us in Coeur d'Alene.
Finley Faith Marie, she was my one good thing that got taken away.

The Priestess Who Sang at Midnight
In The Garden of Lost Souls

Her name is Grace
she appears on foot
walking
through the wind and rain
slowly
in the Garden of Lost Souls.

She snaps her fingers
stops the rain
tells us
to wipe away
the sand
scattered like tiny bone chips
across our faces.

She once wore velvet
it makes no sound.
Now
everything she wears
is lined
with crinoline.

As she sings
her voice rises
above the leaves
and litter.

Love strongly
stay a child
Say Martha Stewart is dead
Do It Now.

The Priestess *(cont.)*

Listen to your hunger
only fear is
parachute white
gold lame
looks good on you.

Accept that you only know
what you know
up to the point
you're at.

On the days
when your brain
is a pretzel,
look for hope
in the sudden blush
of the sky,
a rainbow no one expected.

If you have a bad dream
tell someone about it
Do it with the door open
so the badness leaves.

Get yourself a bottle
of Dixie Blackened Voodoo beer
Order out – Chinese
Dim Sum means
pieces of the heart
Eat and drink slowly
You are beautiful
when you smile.

14

chiaroscuro
(lit. translation – clear dark)

She is fire
with a gentle flame
this girl with freckles on her nose
who was once
a stunt double's stunt double.
She loves thunderstorms
and wishes she could *be*
that mosquito
dancing along the rim of the electric zapper.
She is leaving
a hatchet in her hand
to chase pigs in France
who *know* where the truffles are buried.
"When you miss me," she says, "stand here
in the spot where I have held you."
Her dog Max plays
on his back
in the sunshine
tossing a tennis ball gently into the air
the first German Shepherd I have loved
who is trained to kill.

15

Kissing Harrison

He came to our town carrying secrets
a bareback meteorite cowboy
who looked down when he laughed
like there were tiny pieces of sadness
slipping through him.
I'd just lost my college fund to my parent's divorce
and turned down a job at the Mattel factory
pressing belly button holes into naked dolls.
So with meteorites falling from the sky
and no 'Plan B' in sight,
I followed the housewives and retirees
onto the desert floor
in search of my own piece of outer space.
Every night at midnight
Harrison sat in the Mattel parking lot
waiting for Avalon, a good girl/bad girl
with a temper and a White Brite smile.
He said he liked her defiance, it turned him on
but mostly he waited, because that's what you do
with girls like Avalon. I wanted to be the one
getting all that love from someone like him.
He opened up my eyes to me
said he saw me, or someone like me
in the pages of Vogue
a girl on a raspberry satin chaise lounge
disobedient gold high heels dangling from my feet.
My voice sounded more exotic just whispering his name.
But I wasn't Avalon. I was the girl who helped him
fill the back of his pick-up truck with space rocks
who listened to his dreams of finding a planet
where he could sing country music part-time
and I could get my college fund back.

Kissing Harrison *(cont.)*

I wish I could say Harrison cleaned up the mess
that was my life that summer,
but he vanished in search of planets circling other suns
and women even more defiant than Avalon.
'You won't get married,' the psychic told me
days before Harrison disappeared.
Her three-legged end table collapsed
sending my tea leaves to the floor.
'Maybe after forty,' she said. 'Now put it out of your mind.'
In that moment of fallen destinies
before I left our town for good,
I cried and laughed
stuck with nothing more than my fantasy
of kissing Harrison, wondering if I would ever love anyone
even half as much.

Hands

When the wizard of misfortune is near
we use them to cover our hearts
but not completely.
Think of the autograph collector
who never leaves his apartment
yet reaches passionately for the afternoon mail.
How would we open an umbrella
light a candle
or calm a restless child
without them?

On a cross-country trip
my spirit drained
from too many losses, too much bad death
I missed a Motel 8 exit, stumbled into a farm town
on the day they were resurrecting the ferris wheel
after years of disrepair.
The pinwheels, cotton candy and streamers
told only half the town's story to be sure
but in that haze of pink surrender
right before the edge of night returned
as a revolving wheel on a fixed axle
went round and round
round and round
I saw small hands, blistered hands
hands that hadn't been held for years
grabbing for life
until the sweat
pouring from even the saddest faces
turned sweet.

Home

You told me to imagine
the lights were vultures
"Blink once, " you said,
"and we'll be eaten alive."
My will is strong.
I paralyzed the muscles
around my eyes to stare into faces
the color
of sanitized dirt.
I realized
I was living
a Las Vegas nightmare.

At the hotel
our pillows
were hard
and flat,
the kind
that block out dreams.
You held me
as we waited
for the rose glow of dawn
to return.

Around two a.m.
or was it three,
we jumped from the balcony
of our first floor room
to follow the sounds
of night fires in the desert.

Home *(cont.)*

"Beware the salamander
on the rock," I said.
You wanted
to touch
it's soft, moist skin.

Walking through purple darkness
my bare leg
caught the edge
of an Indian fig cactus.
"Blood looks different
at night," you said
moving toward me
like a scientist
with nothing to fear.
You stopped the bleeding
somehow
as the moon
shot
a twister
of light
directly in our path
its sterling silver glow
surrounding us
like captured rain.

Valentina Pearl

A freak Italian earthquake took everything away
everything but her father's top coat.
She wore it for thirty winters
remaining to the end
alone
a pearl in its own oyster
buried in his coat.

Magic in the Dunes
of Pismo Beach

'There are love dogs in this world no one knows
*the names of, give your life to be one'...*Rumi

We hear it across the ancient sand
a man singing his song of love and loss
carrying a leash, no dog.
We are like crayons melting in the sun
crazy hot, irritable, not like last night
making love to the sound of trains
coming and going in the hills
a cool, salt breeze misting our skin.
Why do we get so off track in love
when really anyone in love
is among the lucky?

We final spin the argument, join the search
sandstorms surrounding us like hungry rattlesnakes.
Away from us, trains pass through carved rock
formed by another civilization and dogs not lost
take catnaps on cooler ground.

Where is the dog? Where? Where?

Astronauts say the earth from space
looks like a tiny blue marble.
My husband dives right through mistakes
forbidden to be repeated
the sandstorm's mockery leading him
to where blue-grey dog eyes wait.

Magic in the Dunes
of Pismo Beach *(Cont.)*

"I died but came alive again," the man says
the dog safe inside his arms.

Night closes in. The hand of the wind follows our footsteps
rearranging the mound of sand
to the way it was, the way it needs to be.

Imagining the Colors
of a Taos Sunset
in the Rain

In this town where street dogs talk
and myth and mystery
hang in the air like works of art,
early evening light gathers magic.
Hotel floodlights underground
turn the fog a swirly pink.
Misty petunias tempting as finger food
bend toward our window.
I am a peach about to ripen.
Sunflower slinkies tossed out of a sky
busy stenciling rainbows,
leap across the bedsheets
like Pirate's gold.
Off in the distance,
hills of amaranth
tease us toward tomorrow
and I find myself loving you all over again.

24

Hopscotch

Hyperactive as a child, it carried on into adulthood. About to be divorced for the third time, Katrina needed to meet her daddy. She found him in a boarding house with walls that looked like the skins of rotted Bermuda onions.

"Do you smoke?" her father asked her. Before she could answer he said, "I just had a lung removed." On the table next to his bed were cigarettes, lemon cough drops and matches from Coconut Willies.

Outside, a little girl was playing hopscotch. Katrina watched from the window, mimicking the child's movements.

"What are you doing?" her father said. The little girl stopped hopping suddenly as if she made a mistake.

Katrina moved toward the bed, pressing her thumb hard against her father's Adam's apple, a self defense move her second husband, a cop, taught her. The scratchy, gurgling sound her father made didn't scare her.

Months later, Katrina returned to the boarding house. Nobody remembered anything, least of all the game she played.

What He Did at the End of His Life

Tucked into his nights of dying were dreams.
He was not a dreamer.
The first night his daughter stands alone in the rain.
She needs to cross the street but is stuck in front of a large puddle.
He walks over to her, swoops her up, then drops her
on the sidewalk across the street. He wakes up wanting to leave
a message on his daughter's answering machine
an imprint of his love that will last through time.

The next night his sleep deepens. He is climbing on the top
of a rock quarry, his breathing shallow, like he remembers
his father's was in the end. He climbs harder and faster
toward the waterfall he imagines is waiting for him
wanting a taste, just one small taste from its ice cold lip.

On the third night, restless from dreaming
he stays awake listening to a cash poor radio station
play all jazz, round-the-clock. He's used to watching the clock.
Every hour, on the hour, he pledges fifty dollars.
Kung Pao Chicken and donuts sound
more appealing than the applesauce
he's gotten used to. He calls a place that delivers both.
At 3 A.M. he wins a trip to Bali. Not one for wanderlust,
he calls an all-night bookstore specializing in travel
asking them to deliver an Atlas to his room.
At 4 A.M. the sultry D.J. who calls herself the Raven cries out
Mr. Man-of-the-Hour where are you? Already I am lonely for you.

His favorite nurse is due in soon, the one who said,
'I wish I'd known you healthy.'
When she comes in with more pills, he shows her a side of him
she's never seen

What He Did at the End of His Life *(Cont.)*

teeth in, hair slicked back, a Johnny tied around his neck like a cape.
I don't know if I'm Columbus or Ponce de Leon or a crazy man in his
last hurrah he says, turning the pages of the Atlas with his chopsticks,
but come, sit by me, he begs her,
be my arms and my legs and my vision
while we create a new map of the world.

The Shadow of a Dog
I Can't Forget

Married for sixty days
Fender Hicks and me,
we thought having the same birthday
meant we were soulmates.
Honeymooners at the Blue Gum Motel
drinking Fuzzy Navels
crooked diamond-patterned curtains drawn.
When the cable went out
we slept on separate beds.
On the roller-coaster ride in Santa Cruz
Bloody Marys spilling out of Dixie cups
we said good-bye.
The dog appeared on our first date
at least in my mind
a little guy with a square face
who smiled all the time.
I see the outline of his body sometimes
sweet against the sheet
as if he's been there all along
as if he could tell me
what follows love.

Beauty

I.

**...She remembers her mother, that face in the mirror
displeased with what she saw...**

Blue boats overturned in winter sand
she uses them as thinking seats
choosing a different one to sit on each night.
You're so tiny those who meet her say.
The only one smaller
was a boy in first grade
a boy with a hole in his heart.
Who is this girl who looks for answers
across a sweep of sea
this tiny, tiny, tiny me?
Liquid pearls fall from the sky above
soft and easy like a fortune teller's dreams.
We are beautiful alone with ourselves
they seem to say
evening snowflakes floating
beneath a faint moon
like fingertips about to touch
a new piano
each sound, each song
a miracle.

II.

**...She steps out of her dress,
stands in a slip of ivory and satin...**
- *From the Director's notes for 'Cat On A Hot Tin Roof'*

She carries a plain, white tote strolling
ballet-style through the pink sand.

Beauty *(cont.)*

A backhanded wind rips the tattered dress from her body
its faded rose pattern misplaced across those long, dreamy limbs.
We are somewhere between San Diego and Mexico
too tired to pull up loose bra straps from our heated arms
as we watch the tour director catch air
in the pockets of his baggy shorts.
He emerges from the sea, Navy Seal ready and lush
to greet this beauty on her knees
the sun can't burn.
Later, much later, when the sea withdraws only slightly
I will imagine him whispering, 'You are enough for me'
in a moment of beauty
as rusty wind chimes muffle the sound
of their lovemaking, the essence
of what we are meant to know
locked in our memory.

III.

…He was so young. The timing wasn't right.
Maybe that's why she let herself be stunned by his beauty…

Lovewrecked by Billy King, there's no other way to begin.
I say his name even now without thinking
as if I could step back into our French afternoon
smell the scent of the roses on the terrace –
Naked Ladies weren't they called?
I was his early girl
the only woman he'd been with
if you don't count his first love.
With Billy I could eat love
from lips prettier than mine
and be okay with that.

Beauty *(cont.)*

I called him 'the boy'
hoping that would keep
his innocence, his touch, his sweet smile
from getting to the part of me
that never wanted
to give everything away.
I remember the steps in our balcony-room leading nowhere
the Paris subway map in Billy's hand as he slept
and me sitting on that prayer-white footstool
needing him more than I wanted. I still do.
A shutter opened and closed with the wind
leading a stray cat toward happy ruin on the ledge
the infinite knot of twisted rawhide
a present from Billy
teasing him closer and closer still to the edge.
Days later when the boy and the cat are gone,
a pretty maid will appear at my door,
Billy's knit cap in her hand.
'For you, Mademoiselle,' she will ask me, 'is this missing?'
I go back to that moment when I was still his early girl.
'What's next for the cat?' I whispered to my sleeping boy.
'We'll adopt him,' Billy said pulling me onto the bed
as flecks of rain began to fall from cracks in the skylight
wet ornaments of pleasure streaming down on us through high glass.

Stripping for Blind Men

It is the one night a week I feel fabulous.
'This is legal cheating,' I tell a friend who watches me
add red rubber press-on nipples
a whip and a whistle
to my opening act.
The men ask me to describe the movements
which I am only too happy to do.
I am Wonder-Woman high in my pink stilettos
I tell them turning in my own direction
like a flower shaking loose from a fast rain.
Tell me what you want boys I say
with a quick flash of whip
against my pole
the keeper of our secrets.
I can take you to ecstasy's doorstep
with the sway of my hips,
the slight opening of my legs
a slow twist, a twirl, a straddle.
I am cat-crawling on the floor for you now boys, I say
blowing a handful of my Braille business cards
toward bodies pressed hard
against the stiff bar rail.
My hot breath gets the men crazy.
'I…am…all…yours', I say
my body coiled like a Diva
in her first full heat. I start to crawl
closer, then push away
closer, then push away
toward restless fingers snapping
me, this mind stripper, who lets hang from her panties
a velvet pouch full of eyes…

Undress Me

His name was Jinx,
a dark-haired Californian
with hands too pretty
to belong to a boy.
I was sixteen, a virgin,
girl-silly from fantasizing
about what men do to women
and what the women do back.

I cut my jeans into short shorts
and cut my tee shirt to just half an inch
below my swelling breasts.
I rubbed the juice
from a bottle of maraschino cherries onto my lips
and put a drop of pure vanilla extract behind each ear.

Memory rearranges itself over time
but the good parts stay.
I remember the Volvo pulling into the driveway
the sound of his voice drifting in through the torn screen door.
As I climbed from my bedroom window
onto the hot porch roof
the strap of my sandal lets loose
casting tiny particles of tar into the soft, summer air.
Gardenias bend toward me
as I slide down, down, down
into arms that felt like part of a landscape
I've lived with all my life.
Jinx was mine.

Destiny of Joy

*-Everything in life is a search for truth,
for wholeness, for love...Anonymous*

Andy and Eddy lie in the tall weeds just below the flight path watching the bellies of planes almost touch the tops of trees. Home for now is a cardboard box they use as a table and two vinyl chairs borrowed from an abandoned homeless camp, a bullet stuck in one of the seats. The boys troll the trash bins behind the Susan Apartments, take catnaps on fire escapes and get cherries from generous Mr. Ping, a grandfather who loves all kids, at his vegetable stand near the bus station. In their in between life, they watch the planes. They love watching the planes.

34   A moan from above spews wayward fumes across the sun like a demon child alone in a wall-papered room with a knife. The plane trembles, dips on its side, then trembles again.

'If I was the pilot,' Eddy says, 'I'd want a butt right now.'
'Whoa, man, shit it's tipping too much,' Andy screams watching the day run out of light. The pilot touches one wheel to tar then takes off again, pulling away from the place it needs to be.
'Less than one percent who go down survive,' says Eddy, the CNN junkie. In the wind's dry wake, a newspaper wraps itself around Andy's leg.

FOURTEEN MEXICAN BORDER CROSSERS DIE
the headline reads.

'They suffocated in the desert,' Andy says. 'All their families got was a garbage bag filled with melted, rotten clothes.'

Destiny of Joy *(Cont.)*

'Or this,' Eddy says grabbing an empty six-pack holder doing cartwheels in the wind.

'I found an osprey once,' Andy says pushing floppy bangs away from his eyes. 'Got its neck caught in the plastic loop of a six-pack holder just like that one. I dragged him to shore on my surfboard.'

'Did he make it, Andy?' Eddy says fondling money clipped that morning from the tip jar at Starbuck's.
'We drove him to our vet's,' Andy says slinking lower to the ground as sirens fill the air. Eddy stuffs the money into his pocket.

'My mom, she wanted to cry,' Andy says. 'But she held it in.' Eddy pats the dirt around an anthill, his motions soft with care.

'I could feel the bird's heart beating against my leg, Eddy,' Andy says. 'I wanted different for him.'

A loud hurt cracks the air open around them as the plane makes another unexpected turn.

'Do you wonder who's on board?' Eddy says. 'Last time I flew, my father was supposed to meet me in Phoenix. Our new beginning that never happened. I was on the plane back to San Jose the next day sittin' next to a buffed Asian chick who said I couldn't afford her.'

The boys laugh.

Destiny of Joy *(Cont.)*

'I think there's a woman looking down at us who got pregnant on her honeymoon,' Andy says. 'Only she hasn't told her husband yet. He's sitting next to her right now eating peanuts and wondering when the hell they're going to land. He's read all the magazines the stewardess gave him and he's thinking he'll get charged way more than he should for long-term parking if they don't land soon.'

'How the hell do you come up with this shit?' Eddy says.

'My mom got pregnant with me on her honeymoon,' Andy says.

'That's what she told you, buddy,' Eddy says. 'My mom says she gets pregnant just looking at a guy.'

'And does she?' Andy says.

'Just about,' Eddy says. 'The day before I left, I saw an EPT test on the kitchen table. She could be halfway through another pregnancy by now.'

'What are we doing, Eddy?' Andy says turning his pant pockets inside out, letting them hang there like that.

'We're killing time until we can go back to the Susan Apartments,' Eddy says. 'Chill out, man.'

'I mean what are we REALLY doing?'

The wayward plane, circling the city for one hour, maybe two, surges upward suddenly past clay hills the color of crushed cinnamon, seductive in the evening sun's glow. Past blueberries ripening and the end of trees. Past two young boys, thin as matchsticks, facing one another in side-by-side phone booths, dirty fingers ready to dial home.

Forgive…Move On…Remember
(Written to commemorate the first anniversary of 9/11)

He tells anyone who will listen
forgive…move on…remember…

He lost Betty in the attacks
wears her name in big gold letters
around his neck.
He knows you can't steal a heart
fling it against barbed wire,
then lay it back down
inside a chest. Beat…Beat…

On Fridays he cleans her grave
then walks toward no address
remembering how much she loved Pepsi
and the color pink.

He carries her fluffy mohair sweater
in his backpack, pulls it out when the pain
feels like thunder trapped under the skin.

He saw her once
staring over his shoulder in a mirror.
'This is not the only place we are passing through,'
she said, 'Love the world still.'
And so he begins again, telling anyone who will listen
Forgive…move on…remember…

The Anniversary

Twenty years ago today
I married a man
I still have nightmares about.

The son of a father
who pressed lit cigarette tips
into his wrists,
he wore long sleeved shirts
even in summer.

No one knew.

It didn't take long
to realize
I was next.

Now at equal points
on the marital axis,
ten years in
ten years out,
I surrender my
long neck silhouette
to the drugstore photobooth's
carrousel of light.
Four cheap shots
fall to the floor.
I'm sucking a popsickle
in each frame.
Cuckoo clocks
on sale
rant wildly.
Once again
I start to taste
the wooden stick.

one strong girl

Her name was Molly before she changed it to Pim. She grew up in Paris Valley, California, a builder's dirty trick, an optical illusion to lure people, quiet people like her parents, into the desert. When asked to describe her childhood, she said it was like riding a bicycle through sand.

On Ash Wednesday, a day of cold rain, she was expelled from sixth grade for pretending to be the priest. Aretha May Albert's parents said Molly, or Pim, pressed cigarette ashes into their daughter's dainty forehead. It was true. Sister Mary Louise Bartholomew Annunciata, whose penmanship was perfect, like an angel's, wrote this in her file:
MOLLY GRANGER HAS TOO MUCH ORIGINAL SIN.

Home schooled, she longed to visit places different from Paris Valley, places with more water than land. She was, after all, a Scorpio. Molly dreamed of Venice. The Isle of Man. Belize. The beaches and swimming pools of Malibu. These were the places she would one day see.

No one in Paris Valley was surprised when she decided to become an actress. On the bus out of town, she gave the mayor, who also ran a successful waste management company, the finger.

Years later, a Paris Valley neighbor, a quiet guy named Del, swears he saw her in an HBO movie. Close to 200 pounds with blood red fingernails, she was sitting on a beach in a wedding gown sucking the guts from a lobster's claws. The guy next to her was smiling, a giant love smile, as he watched her lips at work. 'She had the power to transform him into whatever she wanted right there on the sand,' Dell said.

one strong girl *(Cont.)*

    Dell couldn't recall how the movie ended. He fell asleep just as the sand started to bubble up like molten lava, carrying the lovers toward the surf. 'It was surreal,' Dell said, 'to see the bright orange Paris Valley Payless sticker stuck to the bottom of her shoe.'

A Hymn for Wish

A sunset that was all blood, the dog
missing in the flood.
Wish, the boy I didn't know I needed
my smuggler of tangled hearts
popped living color into this blind man's life
lying with me every night on the grass
as we waited for restless stars imagined
to fling themselves steady and fast against a midnight moon.
Wish let me steal the best life and make it mine.
I love him the way you love cake for breakfast.
Alaskans have countless words to describe snow
and none to describe time.
The mind of a blind man has different tones, it's not our ruin
how can you miss what you never had?
Wish understands the melody in my soul
the haunted echoes released in fairy-tale riffs, my hymn for Wish.
If I could I would write this dog a love song every day.
People ask me, 'Why are you crying?'
I tell them if love were enough he'd still be here.
I tell them my boy is standing on the rail of the porch
ears cocked, the water rising, waiting for my whispered 'Hello'.
'Find him,' I beg the rescuers
trying to describe for them, as if I ever can,
the place where he last loved me.

MARY KENNEDY EASTHAM's award-winning poetry and short stories have appeared in over 75 books, magazines, small presses and e-zines in the United States and abroad. The publishing list includes 'Glamour' magazine, Paris Transcontinental, the Circle Magazine, THE BEST OF Map Of Austin Poetry, the Paterson Literary Review, Poetry Superhighway, muse apprentice guild, Pearl magazine and the Red Rock Review to name a few. Her work has received a Chekhov Award, an Allen Ginsberg Poetry Award and she is a two-time award winning recipient of Literary Grants from the ARTS COUNCIL SILICON VALLEY.

MARY KENNEDY EASTHAM has starred in and done voice-overs for a number of independent films and was recently featured in the trailer for the reality show BLOW-OUT. Her blog THE-ONE-AND-ONLY-MARY (found at Blogit) has been called 'exuberant', 'a beautiful weaving of your life and writing'. Her poetry collection THE SHADOW OF A DOG I CAN'T FORGET was a Runner-Up for BEST POETRY BOOK in The Best Books of 2005 contest sponsored by USA Book News. 'Points of Love', a poem from that collection was a $5,000 award-winner in the 2005 Dorothy Sargent Rosenburg Annual Poetry Competition. From August thru October she conducts ESSAY-WRITING seminars for college-bound seniors called 'TELL ME YOUR STORY.' She raises champion Golden Retrievers in the San Francisco Bay Area.

Contact:
E-mail: marylovesdogs@sbcglobal.net
www.RP-Author.com/MKE

THE SHADOW OF A DOG I CAN'T FORGET
Poems & Prose
by Mary Kennedy Eastham

FOR DISCUSSION IN A
BOOK GROUP OR WITH FRIENDS

WHY POETRY & SHORT STORIES?
Because they can break your heart and save your life; because
they can make you feel like a hero and like a whore; because
they are messy and beautiful and complicated; but mostly
because they ask you to think and to imagine.

IS THIS BOOK ABOUT DOGS?
I'm asked to speak to a lot of groups, usually women's groups
and this question almost always comes up. I don't know how
to answer it other than to say as writers we all draw from our
life experience pool. I've raised champion Golden Retrievers,
having brought 24 puppies into the world. So I guess I would
say the dog serves as a metaphor in some of the pieces. But
really, think about this, you know when you're asked to fill
out a questionnaire in one of those women's magazines and
there are no right or wrong answers, just maybe a small
moment when something is revealed that has meaning for
YOU. That's how I'd like you to approach my work.

WITH ALL THE CHOICES OUT THERE – WHY
SHOULD I READ YOUR BOOK?
We're all time drained. God, I wish I had a magical solution
to cure that dilemma for you. What I can say about why you
should spend your precious time reading my writing is that I
love language. My mother taught me to read at age four and
I have read just about anything I can get my hands on ever
since. I have my snobbish preferences, to be sure. I tend not

to read popular fiction, for example. But I'm open-minded so introduce me to a writer who does things in an interesting way and who happens to be a popular fiction writer and I'm all over that book. The beauty of reading poetry and literary fiction is that you can open the book up to any page and just enjoy what's on the page in its small, condensed entirety. I probably shouldn't share this with you, but I'm going to, all writers have themes, things we're attracted to and maybe even things we're trying to work out with our writing. I'd be interested to see what themes, if any, you see threaded throughout my collection. Please be kind!!!

WHAT DO I WANT READERS TO COME AWAY WITH WHEN THEY READ MY WORK? I'm a romantic and an idealist and I love language. I'd like to imagine two women, good friends, out for that rare afternoon together. If they've read the book, maybe even in a book group, I'd like them to share with one another a particular poem or story that they absolutely love, or a passage in one of the pieces that they found beautiful or moving or meaningful, an experience they too might have shared. I'd like them to wonder, hmmm, what was she going for here? I'd like them to put themselves into a short story or poem and find their own way out. I'd like them to want more.

Sneak preview of the upcoming book,

Delicato

by Mary Kennedy Eastham

DELICATO

MARY KENNEDY EASTHAM

CHAPTER 1

I killed only one thing in my life. My first goldfish. Mica and I were five at the time begging our father for a pet. 'Squishy' came home in a Glad Zipper Sandwich Bag and because I was the oldest twin by three minutes, it was my responsibility to get him safely into the aquarium. He slipped away from me and fell down our 68 front steps to his death. My father believed in Heaven and redemption and that all things exist after death, just in a different form. So I told my sobbing brother Squishy never even knew what hit him traveling down this milky white river into forever...

My brother Mica and I stand on the window ledge of the church where our father sang hymns every Sunday sharing an umbrella. Across the street in our studio, which is also where we live, the Eldorado River swells and throbs around our work, taking it all, every painting, every piece of sculpture, turning it into debris. My brother has always known art is his life. I'm not so sure art can be my everything. That's what we were arguing about when the flood hit. Mica tells me his vision is blurring, that probably it's the rain, but I know what it is. We lost our mother and father two years ago in a fire, and now this. You don't think of arguments or pettiness when a wall of water asks you, no, forces you to begin again.

My name is Johanna Dane. The bones of my ancestors are buried deep here in Dane's Crossing, a cocoon of singing trees and magical beauty hidden like a jewel between the Whitley Mountains and the Eldorado River. My cousin, Teresa Dane, now known as Genevieve Bello on the opera circuit, practiced her scales sitting against a tree by the river. Some swear they still hear her sweet music spilling from the tree's branches. My brother Mica says the river is his prop. Every day he leaves the studio, a sketch pad in his backpack, ready to see what surprises she has in store for him. He'd recently met two new friends - Eva the pregnant daughter of our new minister, carving the name of her fiance into her hand with a black quill pen and a stray cat sunning himself on a small spit of beach. Scrabble, Mica called him. They both made their way into Mica's paintings.

Like a favorite great aunt, the river wrapped its arms around us, giving us a place to reflect and to find inspiration, a place to teach our kids how to fish and kayak and at our saddest a place to throw the ashes of the ones we loved most into its gentle, forgiving currents.

And now today, firefighters splash through the streets of Dane's Crossing knocking on doors, shouting for everyone to evacuate. I hear a rumble inside the church. Wood creaking, glass shattering. Mica, who skipped our swimming lessons so he could paint, tumbles from the ledge.

I dive into the floating world that is my town, am nearly strangled by a tee-shirt floating rigid in the water emblazoned with the name David Marvelous. Where is he? Where is my beloved brother? I swim faster and faster into the flood's dark corners past someone's teapot, a hot-dog vendor's cart, measuring spoons and the morning's newspapers still tied up with string. Each time I rise up to the surface, nearly comatose without air, I come back empty handed.

Alone in a rowboat, sitting on top of a pile of phonebooks, Scrabble floats by. I get only one swish of the tail. He would have leapt straight into Mica's arms. I jump into the river again, swim past a license plate from Super Stars Driving School, the school that flunked me the first time around. I sat in the back seat crying while Mica passed with flying colors. It's so hard to be separated from Mica. I always seem to drift back to the beginning when we were wrapped around one another, drinking in our mother's fluids. Twin souls.

I am losing the daylight. Out of breath, I crawl to the surface and grab for the first thing I can find, a streetlight lantern made ever more beautiful because it has not been taken down by this ugly flood. When I step away, fling myself back into the water's ratty turbulence, it will still be here, waiting for me.

My arms ache as I push my way through more streets, the dirty water forcing itself into my mouth. I gag, spit most of it out, and swim. The flood has stripped the palette that is Dane's Crossing of all color. Even the downtown buildings, painted vegetable yellow to give us a European flair, look morgue gray. Parsifal, a mystic and mayor of the town, yells down to me from her second floor balcony.

"It's Mica," I yell up to her. "He's missing." She pulls me up, hands me some dry clothing.

"I know where the dead bodies are buried," she says. "Now, go. Get out of those clothes. The boat's on the side of the house. Meet me there."

"You've... you've had a vision then?" I say as three boys on innertubes swirl past us on the river below. I can't bear the sound of their laughter.

"It's Parsifal the mayor speaking now," she says. "I'm trying to be practical."

We pass by the cross on the hill where my parents are buried. I say a silent prayer and remember the moment at the hospital when they came out and said, "We're sorry - your parents didn't make it." Mica took my hand. We walked toward their bodies and without speaking, we both grabbed a big toe. In this cold, crappy room with bright lights that burned our eyes, the two of us just stood there squeezing.

God wouldn't do this to me. He wouldn't take Mica too.

I try to pretend something bad isn't happening to me as Parsifal turns down a dark alley that leads to an old abandoned cannery. Through the big, wide doors I see my neighbors and friends wandering through the room, some of them carrying photo albums. They've learned in one day what's really important. Parsifal leads me to the back where they've dug a long narrow trench to place bodies ravaged by the flood.

I am in a ghost garden dreaming into the pain.

Peering into the dark hole, I see Trudy Peek, owner of the ice cream parlour in town and Billie French, the sweet make-up artist who came to Dane's Crossing for a movie shoot and never left. The minister's daughter is kneeling down, a blanket wrapped around her shoulders, kissing the still wet face of her dead fiance. In moments like these, your mind goes almost mad scanning for images, words, anything that will help you make sense of something as terrible as this. My friend Marcos comes tumbling into my memory. Separated from his family by war, Marcos knew more about loss than most. "When your family has disappeared," he told me "it is like dying every day."

For me, in this long line of heartache, thinking of my friend's words, I find a small piece of confused happiness. My brother is not buried here.

Parsifal lends me her boat, tells me to be brave.

I start to leave, then turn back again. "Do you see Mica... do you see him anywhere?" I ask her. "Please, Parsifal...please try for me."

"I see the river's face," she says, "eyes like little shark eyes, just black."

"Go on," I say.

"No...that's not it. I've lost it. I've lost the image. I am so sorry." She pushes me out into the river and she is gone.

One Sunday, toward the end of summer, I did something I never thought I'd do. I packed up most of my paintings, carried them up the three flights of stairs to the attic, sat down and filled out the application to work on a project I'd become obsessed with, a project that would take me to Russia to work with cranes as a surrogate parent, taking off and landing with them, teaching them to migrate with the seasons and return to Russia, not slip away into unfriendly territory on their way to a National Park in India.

"There's an innocence to this land," my brother said when I told him about my plans to leave. "You'll lose that if you go. "Besides," he said "what the hell do you know about cranes?"

Mica could walk through the streets of Dane's Crossing taking in every small detail over and over again creating something beautiful and new. I'm a minimalist. I try to get everything down to its essence quickly. It's on sojourns away that I find my clearest inspiration. Before the river came to capture him I was going to do it, toss my net a bit further, away from Mica, away from Dane's Crossing.

"You can't be too nice about things," Mica would say about my paintings. "It's messiness, the things that make you feel uncomfortable, Johanna, that's where your best stuff comes from."

The cranes in Russia are close to extinction. What if they disappear forever? They need someone, someone like me, to show them the way. I know how to keep a family safe and together.

It is nearly five o'clock. Dane's Crossing is like Venice, all of us passing one another in boats. My brother likes to eat dinner early, paint well into the night. Our mother taught him that. Long before the sun set, we'd be fed and happy, sinking into the middle of our worn out couch, mesmerized, while Mom told us stories. "You must record all of this," she told me handing me a journal. Later we'd put on little plays with kids in the neighborhood.

Can you ever really silence something as strong as a parent's love? That was my journal entry two days ago. Maybe Mica is safe. He's standing in the middle of our kitchen right now licking mayonnaise off a knife, thin slices of prosciutto, avocado and lacy Swiss cheese laid out on the butcher's block next to him.

I tie up to the side porch, walk slowly up the steps, wedging my way into the studio, our house. I'm glad to find the small gestures of our presence still here - the apple on the window sill, half eaten; soap smeared across the bathroom mirror. We're an odd lot, my brother and I, living amidst brushes and tubes of paint in old tomato cans. Candles, crooked and worn, stick up from the tops of wine bottles. And now, bits of gold leaf, float on top of the layers of mud.

Worse yet, if it can get any worse, I step on one of my father's shirts. My father loved white shirts. He wore one every day to work, the sleeves rolled up. He repaired shoes during the day. At night he read Tolstoy and Neruda. He was the smartest man I know. When I paint, I wear his white shirts still.

I hear something. Footsteps in the attic. I run up the two flights of stairs, two steps at a time, the muddied shirt parachuting behind me. In the center of the floor, eating birthday cake delivered before the flood, I find my 90 something neighbors, the Tobacco sisters, Sylvia and Corenna.

"Johanna, come join us," Sylvia says, my mother's quilt wrapped around her shoulders. When he was fifteen, on a dare, Mica stole a car. He rear-ended a car pulling out of a nearby driveway, felt guilty and went back to check on the driver. "You've stolen this car, haven't you?" the woman said. Sylvia Tobacco dragged my brother into her house. When police came to check on the abandoned car, Sylvia said she was all stuffed up with a cold, didn't hear a thing. She became best friends with Mica after that.

"I should have checked on both of you," I say. "My father would never forgive me." I lay his wet shirt gently on the floor. Corenna makes a place for me to join their circle. The lights flicker on for a minute then fade away. The sisters have already lit candles.

"I've lost him...I've lost Mica."

"Yours was a much happier household than most," Sylvia says. "Your mother loved telling the story of how she met your dad. She picked him up hitchhiking, can you believe that?"

"Then drove him the twenty odd miles into town," Corenna adds.

"Your mother believed in fate, the idea of things happening for a reason," Sylvia says. "She felt the same about you being born. 'My twins,' she'd say. "It was meant to be.' "

Corenna, the less forceful sister, stands up, has me do the same. She puts her bony arms on my shoulders and in a very un-Carenna like way she slaps me. She slaps me very hard across my face.

"You go right back out there, Johanna," she says. "Find him."

This seemed impossible to me.

The rain has started up again, soft and satiny, like a mist sent to us to cleanse the air, give us strength. We push on, the sisters holding hands in the boat. Ahead is a bright, glorious light in the old Indigo Inn. Mica and I used to make fun of the little pink pathway leading up to the Paris pink front door with the shaky pink doorknob. What would it be like, we'd tease one another, to be on the inside of pink.

I stand up in the boat, grab onto the porch column and lose my grip. It's become a game, this ritual between the river and me. I hear the steady knock. ..knock...knock of the boat hitting up against the wooden porch as the river sucks me back down. It's the knock.. .knock... knock of tired love and I am not winning. Finally, Mr. Jenson, one of the vicars at the church, throws me a rope, pulls the three of us in. We are safe, at least for now.

We've jammed ourselves inside the Inn, the walking zombie survivors of the flood. A small group is gathered at the Inn's table sewing towels together to use as throws and blankets to help those left homeless by the flood. All the rooms are filled with storytelling. Someone has found an Instamatic camera and is snapping away, creating new memories. Architect Grif Harsh is beaming, holding his adopted baby, the one it took him eleven months to get from an orphanage in Mexico, the baby that until a few hours ago had been missing. A fireman found her sleeping in the hammocked branches of the singing tree.

The Tobacco sisters have settled in, sitting side-by-side on a firecracker fuscia ottoman. "Johanna, your journal," Sylvia says handing me a wet mess. I open the book. My one way ticket to Russia is still taped to the back panel.

"Leave the book open, near the fire," Sylvia says, "but not too close. The pages, they'll dry off and be fine, Johanna .... l just know they will."

As I walk through the swirl of rooms in this crazy inn, past the stairs that lead to nowhere and the hot pink velvet couches glued together along their heavy spines, I am happy to see so many of my neighbors and friends safe and warm. Seven beats ring out from the Town Hall clock tower, a sign that maybe things are returning to normal. Something at the far end of the hallway draws me in, familiar words I heard my father read from the poetry of Pablo Neruda...*The sons of the sons of the son/what wll they make of the world?/Will they turn out good or bad?/Worth flies or worth wheat?/You don't want to answer me./But the questions do not die./*

55

Eva, the minister's daughter, a Neruda book on her lap, motions for me to come inside. I stand at the mud smattered french doors looking in. A small fire burns itself out in the corner. I give in to my exhaustion, walk toward Eva, then stop. Draping back the bedsheet covering the shattered window, a sudden wind slips through the cracked glass nearly knocking me down. This river, this woman without a conscience spilling into every particle that is Dane's Crossing, did she know in the beginning how things would turn out in the end? I want to pull the plug on everything she's done, watch her, as every last memory, every strained lifebreath goes rushing down the drain. Parsifal comes toward me.

"Our good friends... members of our families have disappeared." She holds me close. "But watch, over there," Parsifal says, "maybe we haven't lost all of summer's light." On the wall a lace pattern, billboard bright and certain dances back and forth, back and forth, an imprint remembered from a branch that once grazed against the window's face before the tree was swept away by the flood. "Sometimes," Parsifal says, "God lets us in on a little secret."

I am too tired to even think about her words. I want to lay my head down on the stone cold floor, fall into a long, deep sleep. Eva starts to read aloud again. *Today is today, with the weight of all past time/with the wings of all that will be tomorrow/ today is the South of the sea, waters old age/the composition of a new day.* The fire rises up suddenly, pushing a mini explosion of embers toward us like poison lollipops. Eva puts the book down. Rocco, her fiance's name is still etched across her hand. Music spills into the room, soft and soothing like a baby's lullaby. I walk toward Eva, want to console her, feel her arms around me but something else, a familiar energy maybe, draws me to a dark corner of the room. That's when I see him sitting big and strong in an oversized deck chair of cracked wood, pencil flying reckless across his sketchpad. This boy who never lost his art is still bringing images to light brightly. This boy, my brother.

56

Chapter One of the upcoming book, *Delicato* by Mary Kennedy Eastham was a finalist Prize Winner in both the Los Angeles Writer's Network contest and the Arts & Letters contest and published in Circle Magazine.

THE END

Be on the **LOOK-OUT** for these other books from
Mary Kennedy Eastham:

…**Delicato** – *Short Stories*
featuring the story **CHANNELING AVA GARDNER**
about a young woman who buys a used copy of
AVA GARDNER – Love is Nothing only to find
Post-It notes tucked into the book's pages, presumably
written by Miss Gardner herself, helping the woman with
life decisions she'd been trying to make.

…**CAKE FOR BREAKFAST:** *How To Live*
Your Best Life

This is the book we all wished we'd had growing up
filled with my own quotes and life observations and
quotes from people I admire. Here are just a few:

… Ask yourself this simple question every day:
HOW CAN I BE BETTER?

… There is really only one choice to make in life –
you can have a good time OR you can have a bad time.

… *'Dreams don't have deadlines.'* —Rapper LLCool J

… *'That which we surround ourselves with becomes the*
museum of our soul and the archive of our experiences.'
—Thomas Jefferson

… Find someone who loves you NO MATTER WHAT.

… Sneak out to a movie now and then in the middle of a
work day.

… *'Be patient toward all that is unsolved in your heart*
and try to love the questions themselves.'
—Rainer Maria Rilke

Mary would love to hear from you. She is available for bookstore
and Book Club Readings, Workshops & Residencies. Contact her
at marylovesdogs@sbcglobal.net

Creativity Notes/Doodle Pages - What great stuff have you got in you?

Printed in the United States
81246LV00006B/212